MW01397421

A Ramaḍān With the Prophet ﷺ

Shaykh Abdullah Ayaz Mullanee

www.LubabAcademy.com

Credits:

Author: Shaykh Abdullah Ayaz Mullanee

Graphic Designer: Shaykha Aamina Jamil

Editors:

Raiyan Fruitwala

Humza Shaikh

Ismail Rahman

Ebaad Siddique

Bilal Wali

Ahmed Khatib

Adam Mohammed

Umar Bana

Amaan Baig

Othman Habibullah

Published by Lubab Academy

Lubab Academy is an online institute, striving to fulfill the academic needs for the average adult with small scale live classes in comprehending Arabic, reciting the Qurʾān, and detailed Ḥanafī Fiqh. To enroll, visit www.LubabAcademy.com

Before Ramaḍān

It was the last night of Shaʿbān. The blessed month of Ramaḍān was right around the corner, and Prophet Muḥammad ﷺ addressed the Companions:

"أَيُّهَا النَّاسُ قَدْ أَظَلَّكُمْ شَهْرٌ عَظِيمٌ، شَهْرٌ مُبَارَكٌ، شَهْرٌ فِيهِ لَيْلَةٌ خَيْرٌ مِنْ أَلْفِ شَهْرٍ، جَعَلَ اللهُ صِيَامَهُ فَرِيضَةً، وَقِيَامَ لَيْلِهِ تَطَوُّعًا، مَنْ تَقَرَّبَ فِيهِ بِخَصْلَةٍ مِنَ الْخَيْرِ، كَانَ كَمَنْ أَدَّى فَرِيضَةً فِيمَا سِوَاهُ، وَمَنْ أَدَّى فِيهِ فَرِيضَةً كَانَ كَمَنْ أَدَّى سَبْعِينَ فَرِيضَةً فِيمَا سِوَاهُ، وَهُوَ شَهْرُ الصَّبْرِ، وَالصَّبْرُ ثَوَابُهُ الْجَنَّةُ، وَشَهْرُ الْمُوَاسَاةِ، وَشَهْرٌ يَزْدَادُ فِيهِ رِزْقُ الْمُؤْمِنِ، مَنْ فَطَّرَ فِيهِ صَائِمًا كَانَ مَغْفِرَةً لِذُنُوبِهِ وَعِتْقَ رَقَبَتِهِ مِنَ النَّارِ، وَكَانَ لَهُ مِثْلُ أَجْرِهِ مِنْ غَيْرِ أَنْ يَنْتَقِصَ مِنْ أَجْرِهِ شَيْءٌ"

"O people! A great month has casted over you; a blessed month. In it, is a night which is better than a thousand months. Allāh has obligated fasting within it and has kept the standing at night optional within it. Hence, whoever draws near within it by performing an optional act, he or she will be like the one who performs a *farḍ* act outside [Ramaḍān]. And whoever performs a *farḍ* act within it, he or she will be like the one who performs seventy *farḍ* acts outside of it. It is the month of patience, and the reward of patience is paradise. It is the month of mutual consideration. It is a month in which the provisions of a believer are increased. Whoever feeds *ifṭā*r to a fasting person will be saved and forgiven of his or her sins; and he or she will get the reward of [the fast] without the [original observer] losing any rewards from it."

The Companions ﷺ were eager for reward. However, many of them lived in poverty, so they asked the Prophet of Allāh ﷺ:

"لَيْسَ كُلُّنَا نَجِدُ مَا يُفَطِّرُ الصَّائِمَ"

"Not all of us have the means to feed *ifṭār* to a fasting person."

The Prophet of Allāh ﷺ empathetically elaborated:

"يُعْطِي اللهُ هَذَا الثَّوَابَ مَنْ فَطَّرَ صَائِمًا عَلَى تَمْرَةٍ، أَوْ شَرْبَةِ مَاءٍ، أَوْ مَذْقَةِ لَبَنٍ"

"Allāh [even] gives this reward to a person who feeds a fasting person with a single date or a sip of water or milk (Ṣaḥīḥ Ibn Khuzaymah: 1887)."

This night was long awaited. Prophet Muḥammad ﷺ had been looking forward to the coming of the blessed month and valued it immensely. For the past two months, since the arrival of the month of Rajab, the Prophet ﷺ had implored his Lord:

"اللَّهُمَّ بَارِكْ لَنَا فِي رَجَبٍ وَشَعْبَانَ وَبَلِّغْنَا رَمَضَانَ"

"O Allah! Grant us blessings in Rajab and Shaʿbān and allow us to reach Ramaḍān (Musnad al-Bazār: 6496)."

Since the beginning of this month, Shaʿbān, he had started preparing for Ramaḍān. Before, he would usually fast on Mondays and Thursdays and on the 13th, 14th and 15th of every month. He also tended to sporadically fast for several days and followed them with many days of not fasting. Ever since Shaʿbān began, he started fasting more than usual; only missing a few days of the month (Ṣaḥīḥ Muslim: 176).

The lunar calendar is dependent upon the observing of the moon. The new date starts after sunset, and night comes before day. If the moon was sighted after the 29th day of the month, the night would be considered as the first night of the new month. The previous month would only consist of 29 days. However, if the moon was not sighted, the night would be considered as the 30th night of the month, and the month would consist of 30 days.

The Prophet of Allāh ﷺ and the Muslim community regularly sought the moon at the end of each month. However, in Shaʿbān, the Prophet of Allāh ﷺ took special care and consideration, lest the days of Ramaḍān be affected by a mistake (Abū Dāwūd: 2325). He would advise his Companions ؓ:

"صُومُوا لِرُؤْيَتِهِ وَأَفْطِرُوا لِرُؤْيَتِهِ، فَإِنْ غُبِّيَ عَلَيْكُمْ فَأَكْمِلُوا عِدَّةَ شَعْبَانَ ثَلاَثِينَ"

"Start fasting [for Ramaḍān] upon seeing [the moon] and stop fasting [at the end of Ramaḍān] upon seeing it. If the moon is covered from you, then complete 30 days of Shaʿbān (Ṣaḥīh al-Bukhārī: 1909)."

As the 29th night of Shaʿbān comes in and the sun disappears behind the horizon. The Prophet of Allāh ﷺ and the Muslims offered the Maghrib prayer and went to look for the moon at the end of Shaʿbān. They had not as yet found the moon, when a villager came before the noble Messenger ﷺ and claimed to have seen the moon. The Prophet of Allāh ﷺ inquired, "Do you testify that there is no god but Allāh and that Muḥammad is his messenger?" The villager responded in the affirmative. The Prophet of Allāh ﷺ turned towards Bilāl رضي الله عنه and exclaimed, "O Bilāl! Announce to the people to fast tomorrow (Sunan al-Tirmidhī: 691)."

The Prophet of Allāh ﷺ reminds them:

"إِذَا كَانَ أَوَّلُ لَيْلَةٍ مِنْ شَهْرِ رَمَضَانَ صُفِّدَتِ الشَّيَاطِينُ، وَمَرَدَةُ الجِنِّ، وَغُلِّقَتْ أَبْوَابُ النَّارِ، فَلَمْ يُفْتَحْ مِنْهَا بَابٌ، وَفُتِّحَتْ أَبْوَابُ الجَنَّةِ، فَلَمْ يُغْلَقْ مِنْهَا بَابٌ، وَيُنَادِي مُنَادٍ: يَا بَاغِيَ الخَيْرِ أَقْبِلْ، وَيَا بَاغِيَ الشَّرِّ أَقْصِرْ، وَلِلَّهِ عُتَقَاءُ مِنَ النَّارِ، وَذَلكَ كُلُّ لَيْلَةٍ."

"When it's the first night of Ramaḍān, the devils and the mischievous *jinns* are chained; the doors of hells are closed, so none of them opens; the doors of paradise are opened, so none of them closes; and a caller calls, 'O seeker of goodness, come forth! O seeker of evil, stop! And there are many whom Allāh frees from the fire. This happens every night (Sunan al-Tirmidhī: 682)."

Ramaḍān has finally arrived in Madīna. The Prophet of Allāh ﷺ and the Companions are hungry for opportunities, always looking to maximize on the rewards they can accumulate this month. As they worshipped and strove in pleasing their Lord, they became an exemplar for us all.

Welcome to your first Ramaḍān with the Prophet ﷺ!

Saḥūr With the Prophet

It is late at night, and the Prophet of Allāh ﷺ is busy in worship. He has slept for a few hours in the night and has awakened to perform the Tahajjud prayer. As he finishes the final *rakʿah* of Witr prayer, the sound of Bilāl's رضي الله عنه *adhān* echoes in Madīna. All around, people busy themselves with *saḥūr* and prepare for the first fast of Ramaḍān.

In Madīna, two *adhāns* were given late into the night: Bilāl's رضي الله عنه *adhān* would wake the people for *saḥūr* and allow them to perform the Tahajjud prayer; while the *adhān* of ʿAbdullāh bin Umm Maktūm رضي الله عنه was designated for announcing the beginning of Fajr (Ṣaḥīḥ al-Bukhārī: 620).

The Prophet of Allāh ﷺ delays his *saḥūr* as late as possible. His helper, Anas رضي الله عنه, brings him one of his favourite *saḥūr* meals of dried dates and water. He eats in moderation with his right hand and begins with the name of Allāh ﷻ:

"بِسْمِ اللهِ , وَبَرَكَةِ اللهِ"

"[I begin] with the name of Allāh and the blessings of Allāh (al-Mustadrak li al-Ḥākim: 7084)."

Saḥūr was an important aspect of the Prophet's ﷺ fast. He would love sharing his meals with others and would encourage people not to miss it:

"تَسَحَّرُوا فَإِنَّ فِي السَّحُورِ بَرَكَةً"

"Eat *saḥūr*; for verily there is *baraka* in *saḥūr* (Ṣaḥīḥ al-Bukhārī: 1923)."

He loved having dried dates for *saḥūr* and would say:

"نِعْمَ سَحُورُ الْمُؤْمِنِ التَّمْرُ"

"Dried dates are an amazing *saḥūr* for a believer (Abū Dāwūd: 2345)."

On many occasions, the Prophet of Allāh ﷺ also enjoyed partaking fresh dates with small snake cucumbers. He also enjoyed melon with fresh dates and would say:

" نَكْسِرُ حَرَّ هَذَا بِبَرْدِ هَذَا وَبَرْدَ هَذَا بِحَرِّ هَذَا"

"We are nullifying the heat of this (the dates) by the coolness of this (the melon) (Abū Dāwūd: 3836)."

He would invite others to enjoy the meal with him by saying:

هَلُمَّ إِلَى الْغَدَاءِ الْمُبَارَكِ

"Come to the blessed breakfast (Abū Dāwūd: 2344)!"

He would also say:

"السَّحُورُ أَكْلُهُ بَرَكَةٌ، فَلَا تَدعُوهُ، وَلَوْ أَنْ يَجْرَعَ أَحَدُكُمْ جُرْعَةً مِنْ مَاءٍ،

فَإِنَّ اللهَ عَزَّ وَجَلَّ وَمَلَائِكَتَهُ يُصَلُّونَ عَلَى الْمُتَسَحِّرِينَ"

"Having *saḥūr* is *baraka*, so don't leave it; [eat *saḥūr*] even if you take a sip of water. Allāh, the dominant and exalted, and his angels send blessings upon those who have *saḥūr* (Musnad Aḥmad: 11086)."

He explained that the *saḥūr* was a distinguishing feature of his followers:

"فَصْلُ مَا بَيْنَ صِيَامِنَا وَصِيَامِ أَهْلِ الْكِتَابِ، أَكْلَةُ السَّحَرِ"

"The difference between our fasts and the fasts of the People of the Book (Jews and Christians) is the eating of *saḥūr* (Ṣaḥīḥ Muslim: 46)."

He would delay his *saḥūr* till the end of the night and recommend others to do so as well. He would say:

"إِنَّا مَعْشَرَ الْأَنْبِيَاءِ أُمِرْنَا أَنْ نُعَجِّلَ إِفْطَارَنَا، وَنُؤَخِّرَ سُحُورَنَا، وَنَضَعَ أَيْمَانَنَا عَلَى شَمَائِلِنَا فِي الصَّلَاةِ"

"We, the nation of prophets, have been commanded to take our *ifṭārs* early, delay our *saḥurs* and place our right hands on our left in *ṣalāh* (Abū Dāwūd: 2776)."

After enjoying his meal, he solidifies his intention for the fast. He would advise the Companions to ensure they have made an intention to fast before the entering of Fajr.

As the *adhān* of ʿAbdullāh bin Umm Maktūm ﷺ enters his home, the Prophet ﷺ concludes his meal, and thanks Allāh ﷻ by saying:

"الْحَمْدُ لِلَّهِ الَّذِي أَطْعَمَنَا وَسَقَانَا، وَجَعَلَنَا مُسْلِمِينَ"

"All praise is for Allāh, who fed us, quenched us and made us Muslims (Sunan al-Tirmidhī: 3457)."

Prophetic Mornings

There is a horizontal sliver of light on the eastern sky and Fajr has entered Madīna. If the Prophet ﷺ had had relations with his wives in the night, he would take a bath after *ṣaḥūr*. If he needed *wuḍū*ʾ, he would do so as well. He would brush his teeth with a *miswāk* in the *wuḍū*ʾ, despite of his fast (Sunan al-Tirmidhī: 725).

As the people start filling the masjid, Bilāl ﵁ makes his way to the Prophet's residence. "It's prayer time, O Prophet of Allah!" he announces, and Prophet Muḥammad ﷺ offers a short *sunnah* prayer (Musnad Aḥmed: 2572).

As soon as he enters the masjid, the *iqāmah* for the prayer is given. The time between his *saḥūr* and his *ṣalāh* would be the duration of reciting fifty verses (Muslim: 1097).

The Prophet of Allāh ﷺ stands before the congregation and starts straightening the rows. He meticulously straightens them like a shaft of an arrow (Abū Dāwūd: 663). He reminds the Companions ﵃:

"سَوُّوا صُفُوفَكُمْ فَإِنَّ تَسْوِيَةَ الصُّفُوفِ مِنْ إِقَامَةِ الصَّلاَةِ"

"Straighten the rows; for the straightening of the rows is a part of establishing the *ṣalāh* (Ṣaḥīḥ al-Bukhārī: 723)."

He would extend the recitation in the Fajr prayer and recite between 60 – 100 verses of the holy Qur'ān (Musnad Aḥmed: 19793).

The Prophet of Allāh ﷺ would not sleep after Fajr. In fact, he found early mornings to be a time of productivity and blessings. He would often send out expeditions after Fajr, and his Companions ﷺ noted seeing much benefit in beginning business trips after Fajr. The Prophet of Allāh ﷺ would pray:

"اللَّهُمَّ بَارِكْ لأُمَّتِي فِي بُكُورِهَا"

"O Allah, place blessings for my nation in their early mornings (Tirmidhī: 1212)."

Acts of Worship During the Fast

Outside of Ramaḍān, Prophet Muḥammad ﷺ lead a rigorous spiritual life. He led the people in prayer and catered to their spiritual and personal needs. He taught in the mosque throughout the day and was available to answer questions. He spent a third, half or two-thirds of the night in prayer. He engaged himself in *duʿā* and strove in calling people towards Allāh ﷻ. Whenever he was asked of anything, he would give it. If he did not have it, he would promise to give it [later] (Sunan al-Dāramī: 71).

However, when Ramaḍān entered, he would strive even harder in worship. The blessings of the month caused him to distance himself from the world and maximize his investment for the afterlife.

He reminds his Companions ﷺ:

"أَتَاكُمْ رَمَضَانُ شَهْرٌ مُبَارَكٌ فَرَضَ اللهُ عَزَّ وَجَلَّ عَلَيْكُمْ صِيَامَهُ، تُفْتَحُ فِيهِ أَبْوَابُ السَّمَاءِ، وَتُغْلَقُ فِيهِ أَبْوَابُ الْجَحِيمِ، وَتُغَلُّ فِيهِ مَرَدَةُ الشَّيَاطِينِ، لِلهِ فِيهِ لَيْلَةٌ خَيْرٌ مِنْ أَلْفِ شَهْرٍ، مَنْ حُرِمَ خَيْرَهَا فَقَدْ حُرِمَ"

"Ramaḍān, a blessed month, has come to you. Allāh, the dominant and exalted, has obligated its fasts. The doors of the skies are opened in it, and the doors of hell are closed. The mischievous devils are locked in it. In it, is a night which is better than a thousand months. Whoever is deprived of the goodness of [this night] is truly deprived (Sunan al-Nasaʾī: 2106)."

He would busy himself in many deeds during the fasts of Ramaḍān:

Reciting The Qurʾān

Ramaḍān is the month of the Qurʾān. The Qurʾān was sent down to the world via two revelations.

(1) Inzāl: When Allāh ﷻ sent the Qurʾān from the Protected Tablet, al-Lawḥ al-Maḥfūẓ, to the first sky. This was done during the Night of Power, al- Layla al-Qadr, during the month of Ramaḍān.

This is mentioned in two places in the Qurʾān:

"إِنَّا أَنْزَلْنَاهُ فِي لَيْلَةِ الْقَدْرِ"

"Verily, we revealed it in the Night of Power (Qur'ān: 97:1)."

"شَهْرُ رَمَضَانَ الَّذِي أُنْزِلَ فِيهِ الْقُرْآنُ"

"Ramaḍān is the month in which the Qur'ān was revealed (Qur'ān: 2: 185)."

(2) Tanzīl: When Angel Jibra'īl ﷺ brought down the Qur'ān from the first sky to the world in a period of 23 years. Many commentaries of the Qur'ān also state that this also began in Ramaḍān.

It is now established that Ramaḍān is the month of the Qur'ān. It was sent down from the Protected Tablet in Ramaḍān, and its revelation to the world began in Ramaḍān. Therefore, it is not surprise that the Prophet of Allāh's ﷺ worship in Ramaḍān would circulate around the Qur'ān. He would revise it with Jibra'īl ﷺ every night and stand in Tarawīh and Tahajjud prayer revising it. He would become distant from the world and focus solely towards the afterlife.

Supplication:

Throughout the day, he reminds his Companions ﷺ about supplicating to Allāh ﷻ in this precious month:

"ثَلاَثَةٌ لاَ تُرَدُّ دَعْوَتُهُمُ الإِمَامُ الْعَادِلُ وَالصَّائِمُ حِينَ يُفْطِرُ وَدَعْوَةُ الْمَظْلُومِ يَرْفَعُهَا فَوْقَ الْغَمَامِ وَتُفَتَّحُ لَهَا أَبْوَابُ السَّمَاءِ وَيَقُولُ الرَّبُّ عَزَّ وَجَلَّ وَعِزَّتِي لأَنْصُرَنَّكَ وَلَوْ بَعْدَ حِينٍ"

"Allāh does not reject the *du'ā* of three people; a just ruler, a fasting person until they open their fast, and the oppressed. The doors of the sky are opened for it and Allāh, the dominant and exalted, says, 'By my honour, I will definitely help you, even if it is after a while.' (Sunan al-Tirmidhī: 3598)."

He would encourage people to pray for each other and would say:

"إِذَا دَعَا الرَّجُلُ لأَخِيهِ بِظَهْرِ الْغَيْبِ قَالَتِ الْمَلاَئِكَةُ آمِينَ وَلَكَ بِمِثْلٍ"

"When a man prays for his [Muslim] brother in his absence, the Angels say, 'Amīn! And may you receive the same.' (Abū Dāwūd: 1534)"

Generosity

The Prophet of Allāh ﷺ would also invest his time and money in generously spending for the sake of Allāh ﷻ. ʿAbdullāh bin ʿAbbās ؓ noted that Prophet Muḥammad ﷺ was the most generous in Ramaḍān and was more generous in goodness than a 'blowing wind' of generosity (Ṣaḥīḥ al-Bukhārī: 6). ʿAbdullāh bin ʿAbbās ؓ also said:

"كَانَ رَسُولُ اللهِ صَلَّى اللهُ عَلَيْهِ وَسَلَّمَ إِذَا دَخَلَ شَهْرُ رَمَضَانَ أَطْلَقَ كُلَّ أَسِيرٍ، وَأَعْطَى كُلَّ سَائِلٍ"

"When Ramaḍān entered, the Prophet of Allāh, peace and blessings be upon him, used to free every captive and give to anyone who asked [him of something] (Shaʿb al-Aymān: 3357)."

A Ramaḍān With the Prophet ﷺ

Remembering Allāh ﷻ

Ramaḍān is the month of distancing ourselves from the world and drawing nearer to Allāh ﷻ. The Prophet of Allāh ﷺ would spend his days in the remembrance of Allāh ﷻ and would advise his Companions ؓ:

"لاَ يَزَالُ لِسَانُكَ رَطْبًا مِنْ ذِكْرِ اللهِ"

"Your tongue should always be moist with the remembrance of Allāh (Sunan al-Tirmidhī: 3375)."

Abstaining from sins and futile actions

The month of Ramaḍān is also a great way of gaining expiation from our sins. Its beginning is mercy, its middle is forgiveness, and its end is salvation from the fire. The Prophet of Allāh ﷺ said:

"مَنْ صَامَ رَمَضَانَ، إِيمَانًا وَاحْتِسَابًا، غُفِرَ لَهُ مَا تَقَدَّمَ مِنْ ذَنْبِهِ"

"Whoever fasts in Ramaḍān out of sincere faith and with the hopes of attaining reward, their previous sins are forgiven (Ṣaḥīḥ al-Bukhārī: 38)"

He would also say:

"وَرَغِمَ أَنْفُ رَجُلٍ دَخَلَ عَلَيْهِ رَمَضَانُ ثُمَّ انْسَلَخَ قَبْلَ أَنْ يُغْفَرَ لَهُ"

"May the man be humiliated upon whom Ramaḍān came and went [without] him attaining forgiveness (Sunan Tirmidhī: 3545)!"

Allāh ﷻ explains a major purpose of fasting in the Qur'ān:

"يَا أَيُّهَا الَّذِينَ آمَنُوا كُتِبَ عَلَيْكُمُ الصِّيَامُ كَمَا كُتِبَ عَلَى الَّذِينَ مِنْ قَبْلِكُمْ لَعَلَّكُمْ تَتَّقُونَ"

"O those who believe! Fasting has been made obligatory upon you, as it was made obligatory upon the people before you for you, to attain *taqwā* (Qur'ān: 2:183)"

Attaining *taqwā* is a major purpose of fasting. *Taqwā* can be defined in three ways:

1) Always being aware of Allāh ﷻ
2) Abstaining from sins
3) Fearing Allāh ﷻ

The reason fasting helps us adopt *taqwā* is because the abstaining from food, drink and intercourse allows us to train our '*nafs*' (desires). If a person can train themselves to stay away from the necessary, the futile and the impermissible become easier to leave as well. When this is done solely to please Allāh ﷻ, this cultivates *taqwā* within the hearts.

The Prophet of Allāh ﷺ was mindful of disciplining himself during the fast. He would explain to the Companions ﷺ:

"كَمْ مِنْ صَائِمٍ لَيْسَ لَهُ مِنْ صِيَامِهِ إِلَّا الْجُوعُ، وَكَمْ مِنْ قَائِمٍ لَيْسَ لَهُ مِنْ قِيَامِهِ إِلَّا السَّهَرُ"

"There are many who fast but attain nothing from their fast besides hunger. There are many who stand in prayer at night but attain nothing from their standing but the loss of sleep (Musnad Aḥmad: 9685)."

He would also warn the Companions ﷺ:

"مَنْ لَمْ يَدَعْ قَوْلَ الزُّورِ وَالعَمَلَ بِهِ، فَلَيْسَ لِلَّهِ حَاجَةٌ فِي أَنْ يَدَعَ طَعَامَهُ وَشَرَابَهُ"

"Allāh is of no need of a person to leave their food and drink if they don't leave speaking lies and acting evil (Ṣaḥīḥ al-Bukhārī: 1903)."

He advised the Companions ﷺ to adopt the following strategy in avoiding arguments:

" الصِّيَامُ جُنَّةٌ فَلاَ يَرْفُثْ وَلاَ يَجْهَلْ، وَإِنِ امْرُؤٌ قَاتَلَهُ أَوْ شَاتَمَهُ فَلْيَقُلْ: إِنِّي صَائِمٌ مَرَّتَيْنِ"

"The fast is a shield [from sins and futile actions], so a person should not be immodest nor act in an ignorant manner. If a person fights with him or her or swears at him or her, he or she should say, 'I am fasting! I am fasting!' (Ṣaḥīḥ al-Bukhārī: 1894)"

The Prophet of Allāh ﷺ would also control the amount he slept during Ramaḍān. He would opt for a binomial sleep schedule, dividing his sleep between the night and the afternoon. The afternoon nap, the *qaylūla,* was a special *sunnah* of the Prophet of Allāh ﷺ. He would say:

"قِيلُوا فَإِنَّ الشَّيْطَانَ لَا يَقِيلُ"

"Sleep in the afternoon, for the devil does not sleep in the afternoon (al-Muʿjam al-Awsaṭ: 28)."

The Prophet of Allāh ﷺ and the Companions ﷺ would generally sleep before the Ẓuhr prayer. However, on Fridays, they would sleep after the Friday prayer (Ṣaḥīḥ Ibn Ḥibbān: 2810).

Ifṭār with the Prophet of Allāh

The first day of Ramaḍān is almost over. The Muslims of Madīnā sit around their humble meals and wait for sunset. The Prophet of Allāh ﷺ reminds them to make *du'ā* and says:

"إِنَّ لِلصَّائِمِ عِنْدَ فِطْرِهِ لَدَعْوَةً مَا تُرَدُّ"

"Verily, the fasting person has a prayer at the time of *iftār* which is not rejected (Sunan Ibn Māja: 1753)."

As the sun sets, Prophet Muḥammad ﷺ is quick to end his fast. He encourages the Companions ﷺ to do the same:

"قَالَ اللهُ عَزَّ وَجَلَّ: إِنَّ أَحَبَّ عِبَادِي إِلَيَّ أَعْجَلُهُمْ فِطْرًا"

"Allāh, the dominant and exalted, says, "Verily, the most beloved of my servants to me are the fastest ones to end their fast (Sunan al-Tirmidhī: 700)."

He would also say:

"لاَ يَزَالُ النَّاسُ بِخَيْرٍ مَا عَجَّلُوا الفِطْرَ"

"The people will remain with virtue as long as they hasten in ending their fast (Ṣaḥīḥ al-Bukhārī: 1957)."

At the time of *ifṭār*, he would recite the following *du'ā:*

"ذَهَبَ الظَّمَأُ وَابْتَلَّتِ الْعُرُوقُ، وَثَبَتَ الْأَجْرُ إِنْ شَاءَ اللهُ"

"The thirst has gone, the veins have become moist, and, with the will of Allāh, the reward has been established (Sunan Abū Dawūd: 2357)."

He also used to say:

"اللَّهُمَّ لَكَ صُمْتُ، وَعَلَى رِزْقِكَ أَفْطَرْتُ"

"O Allah! I fasted for you, and with your provisions, I break my fast (Sunan Abū Dāwūd: 2358)."[1]

The Prophet of Allāh ﷺ would not start the Maghrib prayer until he had had some *ifṭār*. He would prefer to have fresh dates for *ifṭār*. If those were not available, then dry dates. If that was also not available, then he would end his

[1] This *ḥadīth* is *mursal*.

fast with a few drinks of water (Sunan al-Tirmidhī: 696). He would advise the Companions ﷺ:

"إِذَا أَفْطَرَ أَحَدُكُمْ فَلْيُفْطِرْ عَلَى تَمْرٍ، فَإِنْ لَمْ يَجِدْ فَلْيُفْطِرْ عَلَى مَاءٍ فَإِنَّهُ طَهُورٌ"

"When one of you ends your fast, he or she should end it with dried dates. If he or she does not find any, then they should end it with water; for water is purifying (Sunan al-Tirmidhī: 695)."

After *ifṭār*, the Maghrib prayer would be performed without delay.

The Prophet of Allāh ﷺ would rarely eat alone. Madīna had many poor men who were known as Aṣḥāb al-Ṣuffa. He would encourage the Companions ﷺ to share their food with them:

"مَنْ كَانَ عِنْدَهُ طَعَامُ اثْنَيْنِ فَلْيَذْهَبْ بِثَالِثٍ، وَإِنْ أَرْبَعٌ فَخَامِسٌ أَوْ سَادِسٌ"

"Whoever has food for two people, should take [home with him] a third person. Whoever has food for four people, should take a fifth or [even] a sixth person (Ṣaḥīḥ al-Bukhārī: 602)."

Prophet Muḥammad ﷺ would eat on the floor. The food would be kept in a bigger plate which would be shared amongst everyone present. There would be no fine bread, but a humble meal of whatever could easily be acquired (Musnad Aḥmed: 12325). Prophet Muḥmmad ﷺ would eat with three fingers and would eat from the side which was near him. He would teach the children to eat in this manner as well:

"يَا غُلَامُ، سَمِّ اللهَ، وَكُلْ بِيَمِينِكَ، وَكُلْ مِمَّا يَلِيكَ"

"O Child! Say the name of Allāh and eat with your right hand. And eat from what is close to you (Musnad Aḥmad: 16332)."

He would also teach:

"إِذَا وَقَعَتْ لُقْمَةُ أَحَدِكُمْ، فَلْيُمِطْ عَنْهَا الْأَذَى، وَلْيَأْكُلْهَا، وَلَا يَدَعْهَا لِلشَّيْطَانِ"

"If any of you drops a morsel of food, then he or she should remove anything dirty from it and eat it. He or she should not leave it for Shayṭān (Ṣaḥīḥ Muslim: 136)."

He would instruct his Companions ﷺ to clean the plate and lick their fingers and say:

"فَإِنَّكُمْ لَا تَدْرُونَ فِي أَيِّ طَعَامِكُمُ الْبَرَكَةُ"

"[...] because you don't know in which portion of the food are the blessings (Ṣaḥīḥ Muslim: 136)."

Revising the Qur'ān

The first night of Ramaḍān has set in. The Prophet of Allāh ﷺ and the Companions ﷺ have finished their small meals and are preparing for a night of worship and exertion. The Prophet of Allāh ﷺ resorts to a state of seclusion and waits for a special guest.

This special guest visited the Prophet of Allāh ﷺ every night in Ramadān, and the two shared a very special practice. Abdullāh bin ʿAbbās ﷺ explains these sessions as follows:

"كَانَ جِبْرِيلُ عَلَيْهِ السَّلاَمُ يَلْقَاهُ كُلَّ لَيْلَةٍ فِي رَمَضَانَ، حَتَّى يَنْسَلِخَ،

يَعْرِضُ عَلَيْهِ النَّبِيُّ صَلَّى اللهُ عَلَيْهِ وَسَلَّمَ القُرْآنَ"

"Jibrīl, upon him be peace, used to meet [the Prophet of Allāh ﷺ] every night in Ramaḍān till the end of the month. The Prophet, peace and salutations be upon him, used to recite the Qur'ān to him (Ṣaḥīḥ al-Bukhārī: 1902)."

They would revise the entire Qur'ān once in Ramaḍān. However, on the year that Prophet Muḥammad ﷺ passed away, they had revised it twice (Ṣaḥīḥ al-Bukhārī: 4998). This extra connection to the Qur᾿ān brought about a change in the Prophet's ﷺ life. He distanced himself from the world and became ever more generous. Sayyidunā ᶜAbdullāh bin ᶜAbbās رضي الله عنهما remarks:

"كَانَ رَسُولُ اللهِ صَلَّى اللهُ عَلَيْهِ وَسَلَّمَ أَجْوَدَ النَّاسِ، وَكَانَ أَجْوَدُ مَا يَكُونُ فِي رَمَضَانَ حِينَ يَلْقَاهُ جِبْرِيلُ، وَكَانَ يَلْقَاهُ فِي كُلِّ لَيْلَةٍ مِنْ رَمَضَانَ فَيُدَارِسُهُ القُرْآنَ، فَلَرَسُولُ اللهِ صَلَّى اللهُ عَلَيْهِ وَسَلَّمَ أَجْوَدُ بِالخَيْرِ مِنَ الرِّيحِ المُرْسَلَةِ"

"The Prophet of Allāh, peace and salutations be upon him, was the most generous person. He practiced the most generosity when Jibrīl met him in Ramaḍān. [Jibrīl] used to meet him every night and study the Qur᾿ān with him. The Prophet of Allāh, peace and salutation be upon him, was surely more generous in goodness than a blowing wind (Ṣaḥīḥ al-Bukhārī: 6)."

The Night Prayers

Note: There is a lot of disagreement regarding the nature of the Prophet's ﷺ night prayer in Ramaḍān. In uniting all the *aḥādīth*, it is the author's view that Tarāwīḥ is a separate prayer than Tahajjud, and they were both performed by the Prophet of Allāh ﷺ in the month of Ramaḍān.

A significant portion of the night has passed. The sky is completely dark, and the ʿIshāʾ prayer has been performed. There was a time when Madīnā would be filled with futile conversations in this hour. However, the Prophet ﷺ had disciplined his followers against that. He taught them to utilize the night in sleep, family time and worship. He would not like sleep before ʿIshāʾ and futile conversations after it (Ṣaḥīḥ al-Bukhārī: 771).

The Prophet ﷺ retires to his home and enjoys a conversation with one of his wives (Ṣaḥīḥ al-Bukhārī: 4569). After a while, he returns to the masjid with the intention to perform his Tarāwīḥ prayer. As he enters, he finds Sayyidunā Ubayy bin Kaʿb ؓ leading some people in prayer in a corner of the masjid. He asks a companion nearby, 'What are they performing?' The companion responds, '[The followers in the prayer] have not memorized much Qur'ān, and Ubayy bin Kaᶜb is leading them in [Tarāwīḥ] prayer.' He responds encouragingly:

"أَصَابُوا، وَنِعْمَ مَا صَنَعُوا"

"They have acted correctly and have done something great (Sunan Abū Dāwūd: 1377)!"

He would have liked to allow people to perform this prayer regularly with him in congregation, but he worried that the prayer would be made compulsory upon the people. Sayyidatuna ᶜĀ'isha ﵂ explains:

"أَنَّ رَسُولَ اللهِ صَلَّى اللهُ عَلَيْهِ وَسَلَّمَ، خَرَجَ مِنْ جَوْفِ اللَّيْلِ فَصَلَّى فِي الْمَسْجِدِ، فَصَلَّى رِجَالٌ بِصَلَاتِهِ، فَأَصْبَحَ النَّاسُ يَتَحَدَّثُونَ بِذَلِكَ، فَاجْتَمَعَ أَكْثَرُ مِنْهُمْ، فَخَرَجَ رَسُولُ اللهِ صَلَّى اللهُ عَلَيْهِ وَسَلَّمَ فِي اللَّيْلَةِ الثَّانِيَةِ، فَصَلَّوْا بِصَلَاتِهِ، فَأَصْبَحَ النَّاسُ يَذْكُرُونَ ذَلِكَ، فَكَثُرَ أَهْلُ

الْمَسْجِدِ مِنَ اللَّيْلَةِ الثَّالِثَةِ، فَخَرَجَ فَصَلَّوْا بِصَلَاتِهِ، فَلَمَّا كَانَتِ اللَّيْلَةُ الرَّابِعَةُ عَجَزَ الْمَسْجِدُ عَنْ أَهْلِهِ، فَلَمْ يَخْرُجْ إِلَيْهِمْ رَسُولُ اللهِ صَلَّى اللهُ عَلَيْهِ وَسَلَّمَ، فَطَفِقَ رِجَالٌ مِنْهُمْ يَقُولُونَ: الصَّلَاةَ، فَلَمْ يَخْرُجْ إِلَيْهِمْ رَسُولُ اللهِ صَلَّى اللهُ عَلَيْهِ وَسَلَّمَ حَتَّى خَرَجَ لِصَلَاةِ الْفَجْرِ، فَلَمَّا قَضَى الْفَجْرَ أَقْبَلَ عَلَى النَّاسِ، ثُمَّ تَشَهَّدَ، فَقَالَ: «أَمَّا بَعْدُ، فَإِنَّهُ لَمْ يَخْفَ عَلَيَّ شَأْنُكُمُ اللَّيْلَةَ، وَلَكِنِّي خَشِيتُ أَنْ تُفْرَضَ عَلَيْكُمْ صَلَاةُ اللَّيْلِ فَتَعْجِزُوا عَنْهَا"

"The Prophet of Allāh, peace and salutations be upon him, left in the middle of the night and prayed [Tarāwīḥ] in the masjid. Some men followed him in the prayer. People started speaking about this prayer, [and the following night] more people gathered. The Prophet of Allāh, peace and salutations be upon him, came out for the second night, and the people followed him in prayer. [Yet again], people started speaking about this prayer, and a great number gathered on the third night. [The Prophet of Allāh ﷺ] came out and the people followed him in prayer. On the fourth night, the masjid was overflowing, but the Prophet of Allāh, peace and salutations be upon him, did not come. Some men started exclaiming, 'The prayer!' but the [Prophet of Allāh ﷺ] did not come out until Fajr time. After performing the Fajr prayer, he turned towards the people and declared the *shahāda*. He said, 'I was not unaware of your presence last night. However, I was afraid that the night prayer [of Tarāwīḥ] would become obligatory upon you [if we observe it with such regard], and you would not be able to uphold it. (Ṣaḥīḥ Muslim: 178)"

Although he would often pray this prayer alone, he used to emphasize its importance to the Companions 	رضي الله عنهم. Sayyidunā Abū Hurayrah رضي الله عنه notes:

"كَانَ رَسُولُ اللهِ صَلَّى اللهُ عَلَيْهِ وَسَلَّمَ يُرَغِّبُ فِي قِيَامِ رَمَضَانَ مِنْ غَيْرِ أَنْ يَأْمُرَهُمْ فِيهِ بِعَزِيمَةٍ، فَيَقُولُ: «مَنْ قَامَ رَمَضَانَ إِيمَانًا وَاحْتِسَابًا، غُفِرَ لَهُ مَا تَقَدَّمَ مِنْ ذَنْبِهِ»، فَتُوُفِّيَ رَسُولُ اللهِ صَلَّى اللهُ عَلَيْهِ وَسَلَّمَ وَالْأَمْرُ عَلَى

ذَلِكَ ثُمَّ كَانَ الْأَمْرُ عَلَى ذَلِكَ فِي خِلَافَةِ أَبِي بَكْرٍ، وَصَدْرًا مِنْ خِلَافَةِ

عُمَرَ عَلَى ذَلِكَ"

"The Prophet of Allāh used to encourage people to perform Tarāwīḥ during Ramaḍān, without emphasizing the command. He used to say, 'Whoever stands in Ramaḍān with *īmān* and hope of reward, his or her past sins are forgiven.' The matter remained as such until the Prophet, peace and salutations be upon him, passed away, during the caliphate of Abū Bakr and the early periods of the caliphate of ʿUmar (Ṣaḥīḥ Muslim: 174)."

He would also encourage them thus:

"إِنَّ اللهَ عَزَّ وَجَلَّ فَرَضَ صِيَامَ رَمَضَانَ، وَسَنَنْتُ قِيَامَهُ، فَمَنْ صَامَهُ

وَقَامَهُ إِيمَانًا واحْتِسَابًا، خَرَجَ مِنَ الذُّنُوبِ كَيَوْمِ وَلَدَتْهُ أُمُّهُ"

"Allāh, the most dominant and exalted, has surely mandated the fasting of Ramaḍān, and I have made standing in prayer in its night my *sunnah*. Whoever fasts and prays at night during Ramaḍān with *īmān* and hope of reward, he or she will be free from sin as they were when their mothers gave birth to them (Musnad Aḥmad: 1660)."

In the masjid, he had built a small partition with palm leaves to enjoy seclusion for this prayer (Ṣaḥīḥ al-Bukhārī: 6113). This was a time when he could be alone with his Lord. He looked forward to this connection and felt coolness within it. He would say:

"جُعِلَتْ قُرَّةُ عَيْنِي فِي الصَّلَاةِ"

"The coolness of my eyes has been placed in *ṣalāh* (Musnad Aḥmed: 14037)."

Sleep:

The Prophet of Allāh ﷺ decides to retire for a little sleep (Ṣaḥīḥ Muslim: 139). He returns to his room where his wife is already asleep on their simple mat which would often leave imprints on their side. His pillow is made leather and filled with palm fibers (Ṣaḥīḥ al-Bukhārī: 5843). Before bed, he places his palms together and blows on them. He then recites Sūra al-Aḥad, Sūra al-Falaq and Sūra al-Nās over them and rubs his palms over his entire body (Ṣaḥīḥ al-Bukhārī: 5017).

Before retiring for the night, he supplicates to his lord:

"اللَّهُمَّ بِاسْمِكَ أَمُوتُ وَأَحْيَا"

"O Allah! With your name I die and come to life (Ṣaḥīḥ al-Bukhārī: 6314)."

Tahajjud

It is well into the night. The streets of Madīna are empty, but the houses are filled with men and women who are yearning to come close to their lord via their Tahajjud prayer. The Prophet of Allāh ﷺ opens his eyes and says:

"الحَمْدُ لِلهِ الَّذِي أَحْيَانَا بَعْدَ مَا أَمَاتَنَا وَإِلَيْهِ النُّشُورُ"

"All praise is for Allāh, who gave us life after giving us death; and to him is our return (Ṣaḥīḥ al-Bukhārī: 6314)."

He reaches for the *miswāk* that he would keep by his pillow (Ṣaḥīḥ al-Bukhārī: 1136). He washes it and uses it to clean his teeth. He then opens his mouth and uses the *miswāk* to clean his tongue, while an audible "ʿĀ ʿĀ" sound can be heard (Ṣaḥīḥ Ibn Ḥibbān: 1037). He then passes the *miswāk* to his wife, ʿĀʾisha ﵂, who first uses it herself in order to attain blessings from her beloved's saliva, and then washes it for later use (Sunan Abū Dāwūd: 52).

Prophet Muḥammad ﷺ explained to us that utilizing the *miswāk* was a practice of all the prophets (Sunan al-Tirmidhī: 1080). The Prophet ﷺ would use the *miswāk* as soon as he entered the house (Sunan Abū Dāwūd: 51). He also used it before every *ṣalāh*. He would say:

"لَوْلاَ أَنْ أَشُقَّ عَلَى أُمَّتِي لأَمَرْتُهُمْ بِالسِّوَاكِ عِنْدَ كُلِّ صَلاَةٍ"

"If I would have not cause difficulty for my followers, I would have commanded them to use the *miswāk* before every prayer (Sunan al-Tirmidhī: 22)."

He would also say:

"السِّوَاكُ مَطْهَرَةٌ لِلْفَمِ مَرْضَاةٌ لِلرَّبِّ"

"The *miswāk* purifies the mouth and pleases the Lord (Sunan al-Nasāʾī: 5)."

Prophet Muḥmmad ﷺ loves this time of the night. During the day, he has the honour of serving the creation. During the night, he has the privilege of conversing with his beloved Allāh ﷻ. Allāh ﷻ has commanded him towards this prayer, and he rises to respond to this command. Allāh ﷻ has said:

يَا أَيُّهَا الْمُزَّمِّلُ (1) قُمِ اللَّيْلَ إِلَّا قَلِيلًا (2) نِصْفَهُ أَوِ انْقُصْ مِنْهُ قَلِيلًا
(3) أَوْ زِدْ عَلَيْهِ وَرَتِّلِ الْقُرْآنَ تَرْتِيلًا (4) إِنَّا سَنُلْقِي عَلَيْكَ قَوْلًا ثَقِيلًا
(5) إِنَّ نَاشِئَةَ اللَّيْلِ هِيَ أَشَدُّ وَطْئًا وَأَقْوَمُ قِيلًا (6) إِنَّ لَكَ فِي النَّهَارِ
سَبْحًا طَوِيلًا (7) وَاذْكُرِ اسْمَ رَبِّكَ وَتَبَتَّلْ إِلَيْهِ تَبْتِيلًا(8)

"O you who is wrapped in clothing! (1) Stand the night [in prayer] except a little; (2) half the night or a little less than that; (3) or increase on [the half] and recite the Qurʾān in a slow and distinct manner. (4) Surely, we shall soon place upon you a weighty word. (5) Surely, the rising at night is the most suitable in subduing [the desires] and rectifying the speech. (6) Surely, you have a long swim in the day (7) And remember your Lord and devote yourself to him wholeheartedly (8)(Qur'ān: 73: 1-8)."

The Prophet ﷺ offers eight rakʿahs of Tahajjud prayer which he follows with three rakʿahs of Witr (Ṣaḥīḥ al-Bukhārī: 1147). He recites every verse of Sūrah Fātiḥa separately without joining any of them (Sunan Abū Dāwūd: 4001). He recites hundreds of verses in every *rakʿah* in a slow manner, pondering upon every word he says (al-Mustadrak lī al-Ḥākim: 1201). Whenever he recites a verse of mercy, he stops and supplicates to Allāh ﷻ for his mercy. Whenever he recites a verse of punishment, he stops and begs Allāh ﷻ for his salvation. His *rukūʿs* and *sujūds* are just as long as his *qiyāms* (Sunan Abū Dāwūd: 873).

This is the conversation of the lover to his beloved. This is the recitation of a person who is connected to the word of God. This is a prayer that we should all emulate.

May Allāh ﷻ give us all the power to live according the Prophetic day!

The Last Ten Days of Ramaḍān

The grand prize of Ramaḍān is the blessing of worshipping in Laylah al-Qadr (The Night of Power). The Qur᾽ān's description of this night pushed the Prophet of Allāh ﷺ and the Companions رضي الله عنهم to yearn for this night. Allāh ﷻ had revealed:

"إِنَّا أَنْزَلْنَاهُ فِي لَيْلَةِ الْقَدْرِ (1) وَمَا أَدْرَاكَ مَا لَيْلَةُ الْقَدْرِ (2) لَيْلَةُ الْقَدْرِ
خَيْرٌ مِنْ أَلْفِ شَهْرٍ (3) تَنَزَّلُ الْمَلَائِكَةُ وَالرُّوحُ فِيهَا بِإِذْنِ رَبِّهِمْ مِنْ كُلِّ
أَمْرٍ (4) سَلَامٌ هِيَ حَتَّى مَطْلَعِ الْفَجْرِ(5) "

"We have surely revealed [the Qur᾽ān] in Laylah al-Qadr. (1) And what will make you realize what Laylah al-Qadr is? (2) Laylah al-Qadr is better than one thousand months. (3) The angels and the Spirit (Jibrīl) descend in it with the permission of their Lord for every matter. (4) It is peace until the dawn of Fajr. (5)"

The promise of one night equating more than a thousand months was unprecedented. However, there was a catch: no one knew when this night was.

The Prophet of Allāh ﷺ and the Companions ﵃ started searching for this night. They opted to make Iʿtikāf in the masjid, lest they miss out on the reward of this blessed night. They stayed in Iʿtikāf for the first ten nights of Ramaḍān. Jibrīl ﵇ came to the Prophet and informed him, "[the night] which you seek is ahead of you." The Prophet of Allāh ﷺ and the Companions ﵃ stayed for the next ten nights as well. Jibrīl ﵇ came once again and informed the Prophet of Allāh ﷺ, "[the night] which you seek is ahead of you." The Prophet ﷺ then gathered the Companions ﵃ and spoke to them on the morning of the 20th of Ramaḍān:

"مَنْ كَانَ اعْتَكَفَ مَعَ النَّبِيِّ صَلَّى اللهُ عَلَيْهِ وَسَلَّمَ، فَلْيَرْجِعْ، فَإِنِّي أُرِيتُ
لَيْلَةَ القَدْرِ، وَإِنِّي نُسِّيتُهَا، وَإِنَّهَا فِي العَشْرِ الأَوَاخِرِ، فِي وِتْرٍ"

"Whoever stayed in Iʿtikāf with The Prophet ﷺ [for the past 20 nights] should return [for Iʿtikāf]. For I have surely been shown Laylah al-Qadr, and I have been made to forget it. It is definitely in the odd nights within the last ten nights [of Ramaḍān] (Ṣaḥīh al-Bukhārī: 813)."

Laylah al-Qadr was hence specified to be in the last ten nights of Ramaḍān. The Prophet of Allāh ﷺ would exert himself in these nights and stay awake the entire night (Ṣaḥīḥ al-Bukhārī: 2024). He would stay in Iʿtikāf in a tent in the masjid and stick his head out of it to speak to the people. He would tell the people:

"مَنْ قَامَ لَيْلَةَ الْقَدْرِ إِيمَانًا وَاحْتِسَابًا غُفِرَ لَهُ مَا تَقَدَّمَ مِنْ ذَنْبِهِ"

"Whoever stands in Laylah al-Qadr with *īmān* and hope of reward, his or her past sins are forgiven (Ṣaḥīh al-Bukhārī: 2014)."

He knew the importance of this night. In the last ten nights, he would wake his family for the prayer and they would not participate in any sexual relations (Ṣaḥīḥ al-Bukhārī: 2024). He would humbly submit himself before Allāh ﷻ in these nights and yearn to attain the rewards of these virtuous nights.

Once Sayyidatuna ʻĀʾisha ؓ asked him, "If I knew which night was Laylah al-Qadr, what should I say in it?" The Prophet ﷺ taught her:

"اللَّهُمَّ إِنَّكَ عُفُوٌّ تُحِبُّ الْعَفْوَ فَاعْفُ عَنِّي"

"O Allah, verily you are forgiving. You love to forgive, so forgive me!"

A Special Request

Alḥamdulillāh, as many of us come to learn about the Prophet's life, we yearn to perform many of the optional acts that we find within his life. Especially in the month of Ramaḍān, many of us finish the Qur'ān several times and perform various virtuous acts.

However, the reality is that most of us have missed prayers in our account with Allāh Almighty. The author would humbly like to remind everyone that it is our first priority to make up these missed prayers. Let's exert ourselves in making up all our missed prayers and fasts, as they take precedent over optional acts. In Sha Allah, this would be the best way to please our Lord.

May Allāh ﷻ bless you all.
Abdullāh Ayāz Mullānee
May 25th, 2019

Made in the USA
Columbia, SC
15 February 2025

53879792R00031